Lacanian Rhythm and Blues

Annette Towler

Contents

Acknowledgments

I would like to thank the literary magazines where some of these poems were first published:

Lothlorien Poetry Journal: Lacanian Rhythm and Blues

Blue Heron Review: Offerings of Compassion

The Wise Owl: A Fly has a Way of Seeing

Poetry for Mental Health: Julie Daydreaming

The Therapist's Chamber

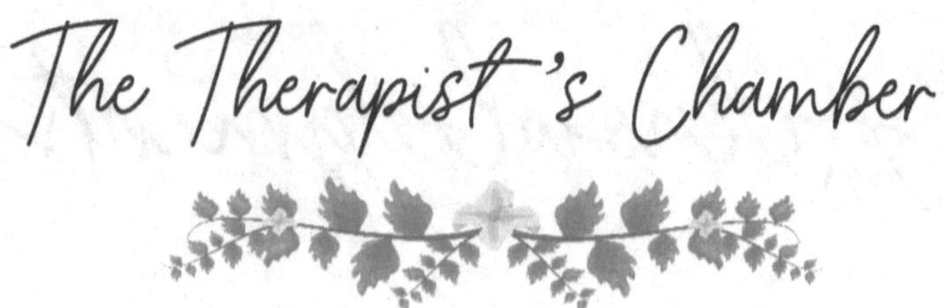

My mind is swirling inside the beach where only you and I are
stranded

And you seem so real to me

I thank the cerebellum of creativity

The dream-like sand trickles between our toes

I tell you about my job

And of a garden where the pebbles line the path to peace

Inside the therapist's chamber

There is only you and I

A celebration feast on the beach

With stones, amulets and shells to line the

Cream-colored sand

2| Lacanian rhythm and Blues

It seems like we are in heaven

Although I am still alive

Inside the therapist's chamber

Inside the therapist's heart

Lacanian Rhythm and Blues

The door is closed and the machine outside buzzes to the beat

Of a noise cancel gramophone

All I can offer you is a listener

With a heart that beats to the soft quiet sounds

Of Lacanian rhythm

And a touch of blues

The dream is in technicolor

Although your preference is black and white

Because in the old screen version

The villain is obvious

It is not you or I

But the silent shadow of M

Nosferatu, the count

Who sucks out your feelings from the

Heart that holds you tight

I listen to your words listening for the slips

Playing Lacan, the clinician's muse

Who sings the love song of an angel

Because I can give you nothing

And what I can give you, you don't want

All we can do is dissect the dream together

Create a tapestry

A carpet of connection, creation, the

Universe hears us, wrapping you close in the angel's wings.

Kohut's Sense of Self

Kohut believed in the power of mirroring so will take you on a
trip

To the lake of lost dreams

Gaze upon you with heart-felt love

You stand in front of the lake, frozen by

Ice, your mouth agape

At the loss you encountered when you were so young

Kohut takes you into the frozen tundra and you glide and skate

On the tentacles of icicles

Wrapped in bearskin warmth

6| Lacanian rhythm and Blues

The empathic gaze of the Germanic philosopher

You look in the pool of poverty

Wanting more and more

The psychiatrist enters through the backdoor

And you feel the transference lift you up into the night sky

Where the moon is fully round and flawless

Kohut shows you

Even he is not flawless

Your parent's neglect and abandonment

Left you gazing at the sun for too long

But Icarus is no longer you

Kohut taught you that your love is true

Offerings of Compassion

Winter in the cream city offers a mist so light that it

Dances on the lake

Ballerina whispers in your ear to soothe you with your sorrow

Gone too soon

It is the holiday season

Children are playing outside with dolls and candy cane

To dazzle the senses

Here you are in your grief

Trapped inside your body

You freeze at any mention of the past

The counselor whispers in your ear

Let me offer you my compassion

I am not your healer

I am your companion on the journey of the soul

It takes a while because time has stopped since

He left

It happens gradually and suddenly in a moment of clarity

You realize that your beloved rests within your beating pulse

A gift from the client

We refuse to take the winnings from the lottery or the cat without a home

Occasionally, we will accept a cookie baked in the oven because it would be unkind to send it back to the owner, who has been rejected for so long

It always seems that the therapist is the gift giver, making suggestions on how to arrange the furniture in a room so that the client can feel cozy

Or the therapist who has suggestions on how to rearrange the thoughts that got tangled in the mind

Yet when we examine the interactions between the therapist and the client, it is possible to sense an exchange between the two

It is in the exchange of being human when you look into my soul and see the scars that formed

10| Lacanian rhythm and Blues

From hearing the stories over the years that make me want to

lie down and rest

I see the compassion in your face when you realize that I am

tired sometimes and that I need the smile of a kind client

It is in the sharing of compassion when you look into my heart

and know that I am human too

Running on the beach, you watch your son throw the frisbee to the other boys, laughing as he runs

You have no need to see him excel or to be the best in sports

Because you know the burden of being a boy whose father was not around

Your father patted you on the back every time you scored a goal

And cheered you on when your team won, the trophy of gold placed high on the wall

You ached for his touch when you grazed your knee

And wanted to tell him how hard school could be

You missed his gaze of comfort and wanted to be free

Here you are now, a father of one, looking for solace in the

relationship spun

Feeling the joy of a father at ease

Because somewhere inside you, wanted to be free of success

That comes with the prizes, the certificates, the applause

You watch your son carefree on the sand

And love it when you can comfort him

Because he grazed his knee on the roundabout

Two wardrobes containing Jungian clothing

In one wardrobe, there is a place for business and casual attire

The grey suit with a high neck sweater

The Japanese grey skirt with matching feng shui top

The sweater dress with sleeves extra long

The sleeves can be clutched during a session when the client cries

A little or a lot

The ego of my day lies inside this wardrobe

The second wardrobe is hidden and is out of sight

It is the armoire of amorous

The glitter of the dress with flapper strands, stretching down

the leg

Adorned with lace filled stockings

It is the residence of the dress that fits the millennial wearer

And also looks good on the body of an ageing yoga beginner

Open up the drawers to find the sequined top, dreaming of

Saturday night dancing

Fill the glass with bubbly and eat caviar and crackers to boost

the libido

The ID of my day lies inside this wardrobe

I bring the two closets together and enjoy the balance of life

The world between therapist and human being

A therapist's medication

The therapist is unable to prescribe medicine from the
pharmacy shelf

Or to adjust the patient's limbs when they are out of sorts

No needles to puncture the skin in this therapy room

The medication to apply to the client is wrapped up in a bright
green blanket

Complete with toy, ready on the sofa that is simple and not
ornate

Because there are no bad parts, I encourage you to hug the toy
with all your strength

Your escapade on the road of Lake drive is forgotten

The constant verbiage of a long-lost novel quietens

Because you discover that you are creative despite the
reverberation of sound

The medication you seek is not in a jar or a bag of candy
positioned on the therapist's desk

The medication you seek is a voice that listens

A voice that cares as you try to persuade others

That you are human and bewitched by the glitter of life

You dream of a day when you stride into the mansion that you
own

The mansion on grand Lake Drive

The Therapist's heart

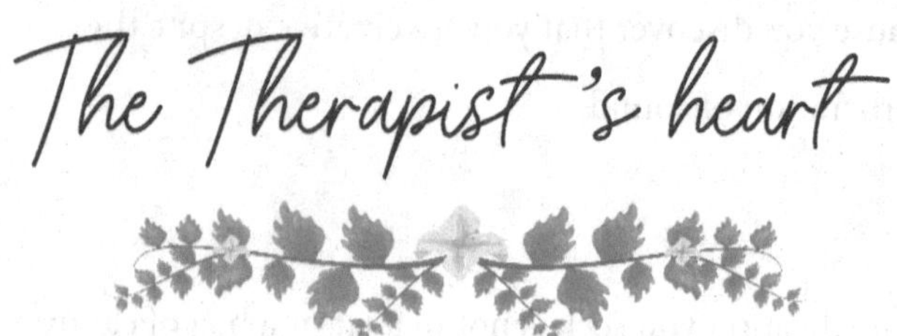

In the therapist's mind, there is a small table near a window,

Overlooking a small square in the city

An opportunity to talk while gazing at the people

who walk past and feed the pigeons, homing doves, and

squirrels

An idyllic scene not punctuated by talk of old loves, or

How death can snatch you before you even blink

The therapist's heart is opening to coffee

With a small Italian cookie,

Two lumps of brown sugar tucked into the spoon

The coffee

Served in china cups, not throw-away cups

Because that would be too absurd

The therapist's heart is waking up to

A stroll along the shore with talk of films

that they don't make anymore

Bogart, Bacall, Lake and Ladd

There is no rain in the therapist's heart

The therapist's heart is opening up to

Compassion and Connection

Mirror, Mirror

As children we gaze at our caregivers wishing to emulate our mother's style

Standing high in heels, the five-year-old places rouge on her lips

Beads dangling large from the infant's neck

Oh to be like my mother

The infant yearns

The little boy stands erect like a soldier wanting to be a military man

Like his dad who served two tours of duty

Leaving and returning, leaving, thankful for returning

The parents smile with warm regard at their children

Hugging, secure, in family love

Sometimes loving, unconsciously neglectful

The mirror gazes back at the child and the child becomes a teen

Teenage rebellion stares into the mirror and challenges the image

With pierced nose and pink, spiked hair

Identity emerges

The mirror never changes

A zoo for healing

The top of the fridge houses a black cat, leaping and bounding from blind to plastic

You are hungover and the action frustrates you, triggers you, torments you

Until you close your eyes and enter a sleep filled with birds and creatures

The zebra surprises you with its long, sleek lines

The structured lines that calm your disquiet and

You open your eyes, nausea dissipating

You want to break free of the cage

Like the zebra in the wild

No more cages or crosses to bear

Because your night of wild abandonment

Ended in disruption

The freedom you seek is grounded in a zoologist's dream

A place for healing

You catch the bird in your hands

Watch it fly free .

Good enough
(In memory of Donald Winnicott)

Winnicott creates a theory of being

He takes a drop of Freud, a sliver of Jung

carves out a branch of common-sense philosophy

Banishes perfection from the conversations

Be good enough

Always good enough

Perfection is not the prize in the

Pursuit of being human

There are lapses, mistakes, errors to make a sheet turn red

All of these downs create human strength

Human strength occurs when a friend looks at another

And says with eyes full of tears

I am here for you

I am here with you

You are good enough

Winnicott applauds the human condition

The right to be wrong on numerous occasions

With wise old face

a countenance of grace

He encourages us all to be good enough

I met you in your dream

Your brain is sifting through the daily events

A text from an ex, the thoughts that you want to vent

Your brain is opening to all parts of you, and I enter as

The observer of your dream

I met you in your dream

It is a beautiful dream full of color and magic

The magic that allows you to fly into the sky without wings

And touch the chimney top like a sweep and plunging into

The ocean like a pelican, swimming majestically through waves
and tides

I watch as you encounter your nemesis at the bottom of the
ocean

A Neptune type character with a cynical edge who believes
everything is

At the bottom of the sinkhole

As soon as your enemy emerges from the angry ocean

The rebel in you soars high and smashes through the plastic
mess

Caught in the coral and you vanquish the past

Glad to have met yourself in the dream of tomorrow

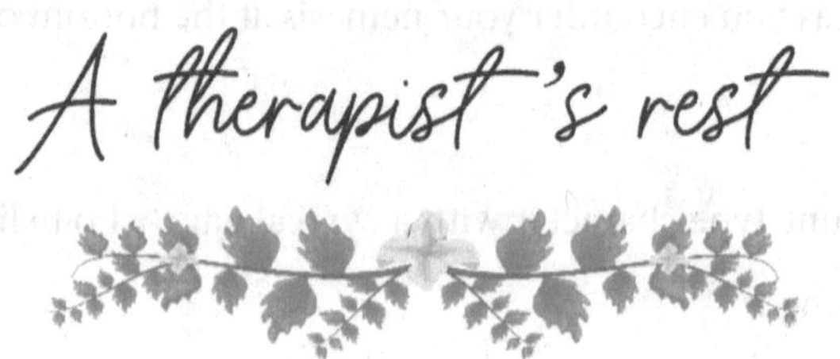

At the end of the day when all the chitter-chatter has died

The songs of loss and pain still sing in this therapist's mind

You take me into a place of reprieve

You wrap a blanket around my tired body

And sing a lullaby to ease the child inside

You remind me that I am human with

Frailties that render me numb

There is a place of solitude that calms my aching heart

A cove full of childhood memories

Of Cornish days and buckets full of sand

A place where no official role is asked for

Only a haven where pantomime characters come to life

There is a resting place for this tired therapist

Who loves the ones she serves every day

A cave for a woman who asks for rest

Spring of Hope

The seasonal affective days of winter are dwindling

And hope springs in the minds of those who lost their way

And wandered into the therapist's room

There is light in the evening and the weather is warmer

Pedestrians cruise along the avenue and pre-school children

Glide along the road on their tricycles, waiting for warm air

The depressive in you disappears into a hole and you want to reach in

And comfort the lonely kid who didn't cry for a long time

The kid that never gets angry

The kid that only gets sad

You feel the lightness in your soul as you walk down the avenue
of life

Springing into the new year, wondering what life will bring you

In the last decade of your existence

And you look up at the sky, filled with sparkling beads of light

There is hope in your steps

You spring back to life

The New season says No to Narnia

Every time you woke up, the migraine pressing into your brain, you wanted to run into the wardrobe

The wardrobe that leads to Narnia

The golden lion takes you into the garden of bright lights and wild creatures

So vivid that it felt so real, flashes in your mind that you can conquer anything

Run an ultra marathon, rule this unruly kingdom

But the headache continues and so you seek a different world where the golden lion turns into a black cat

The cat that gives birth to a bundle of kittens and you watch
them snuggle into a ball of fluff

The hardness in your heart melts at the sight of new birth

You don't want to be in Narnia anymore

Instead, you choose to sing in the choir, play your piano and
paint pictures of a million suns

Give up the substances that play tricks with your mind

Smile at the kid across the road who reminds you of all the
children you have known

A new chapter awaits you.

Normalcy in a chaotic world

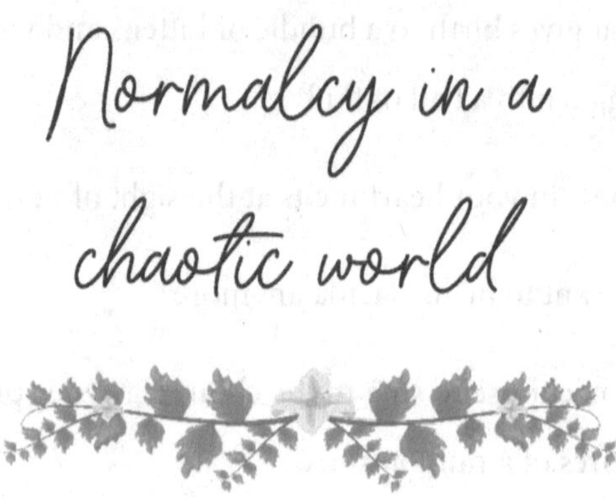

In examining the mind, it is easy to dismiss the playfulness of the child who screams for love

When there are bills to pay and jobs to do

The child lacks comprehension of the complexities of living in a Capitol-raised tower

To be normal is part of the mythology of nations where the value of the dollar is prized

Over the health of the human being, in front of you

The therapist ponders the normalcy of the client who speaks
the words that few dare to speak

The victim who asks for attention after being dismissed by the
neglectful bystander

The addict who hides pain behind one more cigarette

To be normal in this world is a paradox when we are expected
to rush around and accumulate more stuff

In this world there is no such thing as normal

How can we escape from the requirement to acquire more
when we are gasping for more air?

There is no answer apart from knowing that love exists
where there is partnership

No impositions or trial by therapy session but a
knowledge that you and I are both trying to be normal in
an insane world.

A Fly has a Way of Seeing

There are moments in my daily job, when I wish you were a fly on the wall

The proverbial buzz that stays still for a moment and soaks it all in

All the stories and the looks and the giggles that pass between therapist and client

Anger, sadness, joy and jest swirl around the room as the fly pauses and listens

To try and understand the complexity of the human condition.

The fly has the brain of Euclid, deciphering and working through all the problems of

Rich folks, poor intellectuals who inhabit the clinician's walls and mind

Then there is the heart of the fly, pulsating and pounding to all

the tales of

Broken hearts, lonely souls, ecstatic passion and soulful dirge that

Haunt the cracks of the walls and the creaks of the floor

The fly wants to wipe away the tears of those who crack and fold.

If you and I were flies on the wall, I would step outside myself

and look at the stories

With less of a heart, with the rational mind of the fly who just

wishes to buzz through the sky

Yet, the fly has a way of seeing that opens the wise, old mind

The soulful buzz of the fly on the wall.

Bottomless Me

Sartre once said that we have several roles in life to help us travel through

All the houses, offices, family homes, and dens

I have worn several

Educator, researcher, class clown, government worker

Yet something happens to me

When I sit with a client

And look into their faces

I see the never-ending me

It is the essence of me that Sartre describes

To know that every time, I open the door to me

I see a journey of infinity

Illuminating my ingrained feelings

Sad, happy, frustrated, joy

I can avoid them, squash them, choose to embrace

The joy of being me

Little me

A girl born into poverty

With a pulse and heart

Away from society

Table for One

Surrounding you are the souvenirs and relics of childhood

An old picture frame that you covet

Void of a photo inside because

Every time you look at the frame

Your heart races like a dragon

Flying down the river in a boat

With your dad who lost his mind

Surrounded by piano, children, dog and cats

The rabbit has gone along with the cage

The bird cage of your infancy

Tapping still on your chest as you dream

Of a table for one

Table for one with you in a pretty dress

An attentive waiter who winks at you

Because you remember when you were a child

Full of wonder at the splendors in this world

Not knowing that your family

Wanted to take you to cuckoo land

Fall Leaves

You live close to the land of motorcycles and there is wealth in the city

You have little, sealed in your house with too many people

Your guilt arises at times as you try to pay for all the necessities of life

Life bleeds you

Every Monday we meet to take a walk and to decipher all the issues that arise

Both ageing people, connected by a bond

Today, all the leaves have fallen on the sidewalk, and you scoop them up

Your face full of joy for a moment because the air is warm

And you received the government check to help pay the bills

I look down at the leaves wanting to give you all the things that
you need

And there it is

Buried in the abundance of brown, gold, and patterned flora

My fingers grab the five-dollar note out of nature

I hand it to you

Is this a moment of manifestation you ask?

I laugh with joy, and we rise above all the leaves

Floating in the beauty of connection.

Julie Daydreaming

Life has not been kind to Julie

The rims under her eyes speak of late nights and thoughts

To disturb the common man

There is a twinkle in her eye as I reach out my hand

And she clasps it like a little girl clutching a new doll

We close our eyes and daydream together

A garden, a swing, and a lazy cat in the grass who beckons us

To come and listen to the birds that fly in the sky

Away from all the noise inside Julie's head

The noise that comes from electrical miswiring, firing the wrong signals

The noise that comes from

The daily grind of surviving in a world that can be unkind

Come to the swing of joy and love Julie

Remember your human worth and dignity

Dream of a place where everything is valued

Dream of a life where you are free

The Therapist's Fear

There is a fear in all therapists that we might trip up through asking a stupid question

When it is the question you always hoped that we would ask

In your resistance you challenge the therapist

And when you talk about ageing

You see the fear in the therapist's face

You see my fear because I worry that you will die before me

Riddled with physical disease, you smile nonchalantly

Because you have died a thousand deaths in life

This therapist fears you will die

I examine my fear and it erupts into a trillion memories

Of birth, of the baby's first year

I gaze into the mirror

My fear of death springs back at me

Yet, I hope that I die before you do

Because I don't want to write the discharge summary

The note that says

No more sessions

And how can I write that you died

When your soul lives on forever

Inside this therapist's chamber

I hope that I meet you when I die too

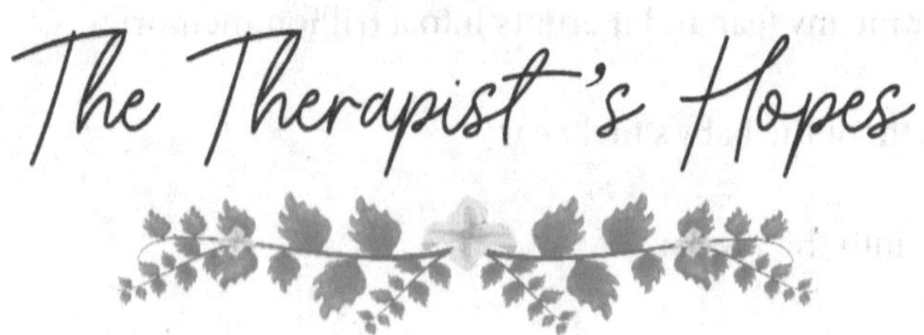

The Therapist's Hopes

Among the screams flying between the phone and the fan, I
have hope for you

I have hope that you will swim with the manatees on a shore
in Indonesia and write the bestseller

Bringing in the cash that affords you a home

I hope that somewhere in the slide between bed and sofa,
that you wake up to the beauty

Of yourself and that you are alive with the thousand chatters
of orangutans who hug you in the night

I hope that you don't repeat, don't repeat in your familiarity

Around the roundabout we go, Therapist, client and a
beloved stuffed toy

You found a dress in the children's section and you liked the fact that it fit

Because you are almost approaching the masters division

We walk backwards and forwards

My hope for you is that you meet an honest man

My hope for the ones who ghost me, fire me, love me, admire me

Is to live in a world that is screaming for passion, devotion, compliance, and subjugation

To live in this chaos with a brow that is furrowed at times yet can screw tight when there is a

Joker in the house, who makes everyone laugh and is the mascot for the millennials

My hope for all who walk in, through and out of the door is for peace

The peace that comes at the beginning of the end

The peace that lasts a lifetime

From screaming infant to enlightened senior

My hope for all is to walk in delight

Biography

I was born in England and moved to the United States in the early 1990s. I enjoy my job as a therapist and in my spare time I like to run. I live in an old house in Milwaukee and have a sweet cat called Marsha. I have written romance and mystery novels and poetry chapbooks. My poetry has appeared in Lothlorien Poetry Journal, Blue Heron Review, The Wise Owl, and Verse-Virtual.